Black Fairy Tales

by Chin-Yer

Table of Contents

Author Biography

Chin-yer, the director of the Maya Baraka Writers Institute, a writing program for 45-60 youth poets, is a multi-award winning poet, fiction writer, essayist, and creative writing teacher. She won her first major writing competition when she was six years old. She has been featured in various literary journals and magazines and her poetry has been showcased on Fox 45. She is a two-time recipient of the prestigious Adele V. Holden creative writing prize/award; awarded to a writer who "demonstrates an understanding of craft, distinct literary vision, and voice". She was the recipient of the Academic Excellence award in Adolescent Literature through the English Department of Morgan State University. Chin-yer has performed her poetry in various modes at Baltimore Soundstage, Nowchild Soundstage, Walters Art Museum, African Heritage Festival, The University of Baltimore and as a feature at countless art venues and events. She holds a degree in Literature and Language Arts and is currently completing her Masters degree in Creative Writing at Morgan State University and completing a creative writing program at UCLA. She is also the founder and director of the 'The Baltimore Scene' arts movement which has curated over 50 literary and art events over the last twelve years including the largest and most reputable competitive poetry event on the East Coast, "Word War". She is honored to be the "poetry mother"/mentor of Baltimore City's international youth poetry champions. She is eternally thankful to be the biological mother and writing coach of two exceptionally talented National poets, Soul and Lovey.

Foreword by D. Watkins

We need Chin-yer!

"Yo Watkins," a short frumpy guy in big frames at the campus bookstore yelled, "I love your writing, it cuts right to the soul!"

"Thank you man," I said, shaking his child sized hand, "I'm honored."

I exited the store, and the same dude came charging behind me, "Watkins, I run a program at the county jail, would you be interested in swinging by for a poetry workshop? Oh and by the way my name is Jonathan."

I told Jonathan yes, because that's my job. Writing and book talks at fancy colleges are cool, but I've made 100's of visits to jails, youth programs and underfunded schools–– that's where my heart is. We traded info, and he sent me some dates.

About a month later I walked into jail twenty or so minutes early. They organized the inmates and moved them into a small classroom before I was escorted back. A round of applause greeted me when I enter the room.

"Thank you for coming!" they cheered.

"Don't clap for me," I said, waving off the thank yous, "We have work to do!"

I gave small pep talk before different students started presenting their writing, and it was really good as I thought it would be. The problem is that everything I heard was personal essay, no one read any poetry.

"What of kind of poetry workshop has no poetry?" I asked the group.

They all started telling me how the poetry books they had access to were trash–– unrelatable and full of content they had zero interest in. I asked the guard could I borrow his cell as I had to leave mine in the car, he told me that was illegal but said, "Jonathan can let you use his."

The CO paged Jonathan and he came in with his phone. I started googling some of the best poems from Langston Hughes, Claude McKay, Maya Angelou and other poets I thought the guys could relate to. And then I started pulling up rap lyrics from Jay Z, J Cole and Kendrick–– the class went crazy. They didn't fully understand how connected rap was to poetry as it is poetry and I couldn't wait to use that same lyrical art as a vehicle for telling their stories. I didn't get a chance to pull up any contemporary poets, but I am definitely bringing in the work of Chin-yer the next time I teach that class because she bridges the gap.

Chin-yer connects the brilliance of Angelou and Hughes with the contemporary relevance of Jay-z and Kendrick Lamar. Her voice is exactly what the genre needs in addition to being powerful enough to attract new writers and get them excited about the art of poetry.

Black Fairy Tales is a perfect example–– it's an addictive cocktail of the streets, creativity, and craft that will not only entertain you, but get you excited about the art. Books like Black Fairy Tales make me proud to be a writer and I'm glad that world will be inspired by it as well.

Cinderella

I never believed in magic until I
watched my cousin transform into a crackhead
I grew up reading of the fairy dust
that seemed to shoot out of the wands of witches and
fairy godmothers
now I wondered if the white shapes that bounced off
The black sticks
had been
Crack
As I watched what had been our city's Cinderella
Transform to someone wearing rags
Holding a glass pipe
like a glass slipper
Face covered with dirt before midnight
Her neck and wrist once covered in pearls
Now she walks the streets,
the collector of a different white rock
 wearing clothes, scraps
four times her size or
maybe her body
Had shrunk
She was now one of Snow white's favorite dwarfs
kneeled at half her size
Top of her head facing a strange man's waist
My friends had told me one day when I wasn't prepared
That she would do anything for a hit of the pipe
I remember how fast she used to walk
Up and down the street, hands filled with
Stolen CDs for resale
Carrying em up and down the block, swinging them like

dumbbells
The way she used to hold her school books years prior

I never believed in magic until I saw how
Our street's evil white queen put a spell on her
There is no ghost scarier than crack, once it possesses
Your loved one

Three Little Pigs

3 little pigs blew his house down in a raid like wolves
As my friend huffed and puffed in his den
The police rammed through his front door
Even though his house was built from bricks
Kilos of drugs
builds his house of straws
He resisted arrest right before
His storytime abruptly ended
five chapters early when the cop shot him while
his hands were up
Tyreke sold drugs to feed his two little sisters after his mother
OD'd
Some cities and some men never live happily ever after

Jon Jon and His Giant Beanstalk

Uncle Jon Jon said his wee wee was a crazy straw
I said 'I ain't never seen a straw that big before'
When he sat it in front of me
He told me it was a special one, magical
That is why it grew out his body
Well, I ain't like the juice
that came out of that thing
Too slimy
He said it was like chocolate milk
must have been spoiled
It was lumpy and nasty like when
My brother KJ left my La La yogurt on the table and made me
taste it
but I ate it anyway and licked his straw clean
Like he said
So I could be a good girl
Mama always told me to listen to my elders
Every afternoon when my papa left for work
He came
in my room for playtime
One time, I was having a
Tea party with my stuffed animals and
My pink teddy bear sipped from her tiny silver cup
And I sipped from Uncle Jon Jon's thick brown crazy straw and
This time he said he wanted to sip me up too
He put his big brown crazy straw in me
It hurt me a lot
I got boo boos down where he put it
I don't like Uncle Jon Jon
I told mama not to leave me home with him no mo'

She told me to stay in a child's place
She musta meant on the floor in the kitchen cuz that's
Where Uncle Jon Jon always told me to lay down so we can
play crazy straws
Do other little girls
play crazy straws with their families too?
I wanna ask Betty or Evelyn
But Uncle Jon Jon said
I have to keep the game a secret. I don't know why.
The yellow crazy straw Mama got me from Pathmark
Broke. I can't even use it
But Uncle's one always work.
God,
Mama said you can see everything.
She said you can even walk on water
Jesus, can you walk on Uncle Jon Jon's crazy straw
And break it? Pretty please?
I don't want to play with him no more.

Now I Know My ABCs: (My Hood from A-Z)

Air smells like teenage prostitution
Black happy babies who don't know they will die soon crawling
over glass
Crackheads selling microwaves too heavy for their disappearing
frame
Drug dealers who would have been pharmacists had they lived in
the hills
Energized policemen who live in other states policing our families
as strangers
Five dollars, the going rate for a tiny plastic bag of white death
Gunshots whiz through the air, the children think the bullets are
"birds"
"Has-been" pimps slick back their hair with their palm
Incest hides crouched down in the hallway, on the third floor, we
all pretend not to see him
Jails never see him either
Kids grow up and blame themselves for their own rape
Landlord knocks Granny's door for his three-week-late rent
Mamas straighten their Nene's hair for church the next morning
Nineteen ninety nine, by Prince blasting out the speakers, we think
that year will never come
Oxygen is suffocating
Pastor is cheating
Questions like "Why did God let Ray die when he was only 12"
don't get answered
Robbers steal TVs in broad daylight cuz
"Snitches get stitches"
Teenagers in gangs get more respect than senior citizens
Unified by their need to stay alive

Vilified by their own neighbors who knew them since they were
two
White people are noticeably missing, like the row houses
noticeably missing windows, and the city missing mercy
Xeroxed frown lines on everybody's faces
Yesterdays and more yesterdays everyone wants to forget.
Zinc souls, hardened, trapped in brickstone

Black Boy Magic

I once knew a young black Joker
Named Jack.
Skin dark as Spades.
His streets held him and his friends
tight in their palm
Like poker players hold their pairs
and late at night
It's like
Our block takes the stage and says to death
"Pick a card, ANY card."
Death pulled Jack from
His deck
Hood entertainment.
We call it Black Boy Magic
Black teens are laughing with us
then poof!
They disappear.
Lives sawed in half
Sagging jeans look like magician robes.
Bullets kiss our princes and transform them
Into corpses
Black Boy Magic
The shows are so sold out and
so commonplace that people don't even look up from their phones
to watch their souls leave their bodies
The streets feel like an enchanted haunted forest.
We all feel wrapped in a black sorcerer's cape and
You can see the black boy spirits fly above the city
Zipping through the air like wizards on broomsticks

I sit here rearranging these words trying to create a spell to break the hex.
Black Boy Magic
Black Boy Magic
Black Boy Magic

Disney Princesses

My friend's older brother fondled my vagina with the boldness and
dexterity he used to play his atari video game the afternoon before.
I was only 7 in the 2nd grade.
He was 14 or so
I remember feeling like my friend's monopoly board.
Flat faced, still
As her brother's cold piece moved over me
He cupped my nipples in his palms and shook them clumsily and
fiercely like dice
And acquired me as one of his properties
Looking back, I wish I had the courage to flip over the board like I
did when my cousins beat me at the game
But I just laid there as he beat himself as if this was a game
My eyes closed
Pretending to sleep
That way he wouldn't think I wanted him there next to me on the
tough sofa bed.
If I closed my eyes, I wouldn't have to try to fight a fight I knew I
would never win.
I pressed my legs togethers as his fingers pressed into me
Moving them fast and rough like my dark body was his video game
joystick
Then he placed my tiny hands on HIS
Huge black joystick
He played with my unwrapped Xbox with his wireless controller.
I blacked out.
Like channel 4 on the TV screen in front of us
As I waited for him to play this next video game but he decided to
play with my body instead

I never slept over there again.
I never told my friend or my parents why.
Recently, decades later, I found out that he was arrested for raping his own child.
I feel guilty for never telling this story until just
Now
I am mad that I probably feel much more guilty for my silence
than he does for violating his child and me.
Moral to the poem
Be careful where you send your daughters to sleep over.
While they zip themselves up in their Disney Princess sleeping bags
They may be zipping themselves up in secrets you may never learn
Or want to learn
That was not the only time I was touched by a boy at a sleepover.

Sleeping Beauty

The project bricks of her home was the same color as the skin
of most of her neighbors who lived there.
She wondered if this was a coincidence.
She stared at her friend's boxers as they swung side to side like
poverty in the humid air outside
She sat on her hot steps
While her mama parted and plaited her shiny hair the color of
guns.
She daydreamed.
Her goals were big like the long rectangular boxes of government
cheese on her grandmother's counter.
Her name was Amy.
She wanted to be a supermodel.
She had the looks and the height for it.
You could tell even when she was little.
Her eyes were piercing, small thin, almond shaped like bullets
Her face oval shaped and exotic
She looked like she was the mixed child of Mr. Lee from the
Korean corner store and dark skin Ms. Johnson who worked at the
Dry Cleaners.
We all called her chinky eyed but
She was beautifully black like the rest of us.
She ended up winning a couple pageants in our community. There
was talk of her getting discovered.
I wish this had a happy ending.
Amy met and fell in love with a man.
A man sweet and toxic
Like the purple Kool Aid made by her little sister.
Sexy and seductive as the streets of Newark.
He spoiled her.

Literally.
He was a drug addict. I am not even sure which drug.
I learned he existed only after she had already died from the overdose.
Her mother sent me a
picture of her laying in her casket.
She still looked like a supermodel.

The Fairy Tale's Soundtrack

A 17 year old rapper was shot two times
Chest and his stomach
He lays on the floor
The holes in him make him look like
my favorite scratched up Hip Hop Cassette tape
I imagine putting pencils in his wounds
To reel the dark blood back inside him
Like how I return the messy black tape
To my Big Daddy Kane album.
Make him playable again.
My tears are thick and heavy like his studio wires.
His mother dives to the ground head first
Like a B-Girl
Her grief
Break dancing on dirty cardboard and glass.
Her screams "Oh My God"
Playback, repeat, playback repeat
As if someone was there DJ'ing her anger
And her shock on two turntables.
Mixing it with the sirens.
amplified
Manny wanted to be signed to a label
I stare at the label with his last name and first initial
Dangling from his dead toe at the hospital.
I watch him. He is so black and silent
and large

Like the unhooked speakers
In his basement that his music played through
Every time I listen to Hip Hop
I remember how his death looked like one of my favorite cassette
tapes.

Annie and Her Chocolate Factory

Annie Johnson owns her own body shop.
She sells her body parts, three for the price of one date.
Her love life is always the car crash waiting to happen.
Penis pile up, rotten cum collisions and
She prides herself at being an expert in hiding the damage they
bring her
She masks the dents in her soul
With fresh coats of red lipstick
And black mascara
If you stare hard enough you can see the stripped
chips on her shoulder
Men only see her as their junk outlet
She rides them on all fours
Carrying dead weight
Like a hearse
Until she breaks down
Until her body collapses.
Annie Johnson owns her own body shop

Goldilocks

Light Skin Dwayne called me "mud-face" again
Said my skin was the color of his dookie
And that the hair coming out of my 3 ponytails looked wild and
hard to manage
Like our neighbor Miss Wilken's three bad ass kids
God,
"Why did you make me so dark and ugly?"
White and light pink is everyone's favorite color
All the barbie dolls and cabbage patch kids
at my best friend's house are a mixture of the two.
I want to be white and pink like them dollies
The only thing white on me is my teeth
I try to smile and laugh as wide as possible
All the time
so my teeth can eat up this brown in my face
I hope the tooth fairy don't take no more of my whiteness away.
I stick out my tongue and pretend it's my lips
So I can look like Anna Roberts
She sits in the back of me in Spelling Class
Lips the color of my new pencil eraser
Her skin the color of breakfast grits
She reminds me of Goldilocks
Her yellow hair strands are perfectly lined up, side by side, like
uncooked spaghetti
Her hair looks nothing like mine
My afro looks like the fur
Of the black cat that mama said is bad luck
Or the black of the tail of the stinky skunk that everyone runs
from.

Do you think if I smile a whole lot
People will like me?
Will I be beautiful?
Can I smile the darkness away.
Mommy always says that I am beautiful
on the inside
Am I beautiful on the inside
because my bones are white?
Why is white and pink everyone's favorite color?

Little Red Riding Hood:
Autobiography of A Hoodie

I knew the moment that I was made that I would be soaked in his blood. I never last long. When I was sewn, I asked that I be dyed black to match the boy who dies black with me on his back. I wanted to cover Yo up like a God, like the night's sky. We would be dark together. Then when his skin rips while my cotton rips, his wounds won't show. The color red over black doesn't bleed through. The tears in my seams wiped the tears of his team. His mom stared down on me angrily as if I killed her dreams. She thinks back to when her little boy was tiny, small, crawling, safe in his crib. I think back when I was folded, safe, in my factory box. Now, I am here, tossed back safe in this box. My ripped fabric will last much longer than his 15 year old flesh will. I embraced his body longer than his mother can. As I sit here, in this stack of evidence, knowing I will never be bothered again; I remember the bullets that went through him and me. I screamed louder than when the needles of that sewing machine put me together. No one heard me screaming for us both when we were hit. No one heard him screaming either. I am still warm. He is not. I can tell my story. He cannot.

Blowing Bubbles

A little black boy told me that
Black men remind him of
Bubbles
Beautiful, effervescent, comforting, glowing
But
Temporary
and fragile
And that
He watches them move around him
and he wonders if they know how little time they have here.
He wonders if God only blows bubbles
For recreation

Nursery Rhymes for Black Men

Don't cry!
Play rough!
Fight back!
Be tough!
Go to work!
Delay your dream!
Be responsible!
Provide for your queen!
Sacrifice!
Pay the price!
Chase your lover!
Make her your wife!
Never look scared!
Even when you are!
Don't let your fears
Break your spirit apart!
Be strong!
Admit you're wrong!
Keep your game face!
Win the rat race!
Respect the police !
Be polite!
Don't move too suddenly!
So they won't take your life!
But still pretend!
That you will never bend!
Your children are watching!
On you they depend
So Don't crash!
Don't burn!

Wanna run away?
U turn!
Even when
you need to rest
Flex those muscles!
Do your best!
Don't cry!
Play rough!
Fight back!
Be tough!
This is what our black men hear
from the time that they're five
Black man I just want to say I salute you
For shining through rough times
For carrying a weight
That most don't recognize.
This is dedicated
to all whom it applies.

Ashes, Ashes, We All Fall Down

A homeless man went viral on Facebook live
Ole Greg stood outside of the McDonald's on Broad St.
Skin, clear and brown like the whiskey in his bottle
Hair, white-gray, like the cigarette ashes he littered the floor with
The whites of his eyes yellowed like the urine he reeked of
jaundiced.
"Excuse me ma'am, can you spare some change?"
Thirty year old Nora could smell the Newports in his breath
She speedily walked past him like she did every morning
Ole Greg heard her whispering into her iPhone
"Girl, here he go again
He been asking for a dollar on this same block for years
He needs to get a damn job like the rest of us!
He got the nerve to have on nice sneakers too?
and he supposed to be homeless! And he drinking
Girl, I ain't got time."
Ole Greg moved from his post by the drive thru and
walked after her and tapped her holding one of his sneakers in his
hands
high above her head.
"Ma'am" he said
in a voice thick and scratchy like his facial hair.
She flinched
"Someone donated these sneakers to me.
Point me to the place
Where I can trade in these white sneakers for a white fence and a
brick home
Or you saying I'm supposed to be homeless and shoeless too?
And why you worrying
bout what I'm drinking?

If you slept out here everyday, you'd be drinking too. You
probably have had a drink before
even when you had a place to lay your head."
Nora pulled out her phone and taped him
And spoke to her fb friends
"Look at this fool y'all. He think he's about to take my hard earned
money from me?"
Ole Greg is now a trending topic on social media
Over
100,000 views
And still he only owns that one pair of shoes
Nora never deleted the video
Even after her boss deleted her job.
After three missed rental payments
Nora got evicted
She moved in with her homegirl.
Now, every morning she begs God for change from her post on the
sofa bed.

Winter Wonderland (Haiku)

Black boy face down in
His own cocaine. He's ice cold.
Our ghetto's snowman

Unicorns

Black poets are often told not to speak about the Black experience
Too much
"Write about something pretty
Or sweet
Write about smiles and summertime.
Sugar and spice
Unicorns, tickles, and giggles, castles, and sea shores and seashells
Write about
Rainbows, balloons, and bunnies."
They say
As if
Black poets actually want to smear the black letters of their white
page with more little black
boy blood
As if we want to
Format our lines
In the shapes of crime scenes
As if we want to find another metaphor
For the funerals of children
Or for bullets
Do you know how badly some black poets wish they could write a
whole book
Filled with poems
that only described
Frogs, wheelbarrows, and horse carriages
Like some of the white poets do?
How do you write about nature
When police sirens are your street's crickets?
And when the only grasshopper you have ever seen
Is the innocent black man who ran for his life

In your neighbor's yard
Right before he was shot by the police?
I will write about peace
When you fight for mine
I will write about flowers
When I stop buying them for the mothers
Who have lost their 13 year old sons.

The Enchanted Ball

Huge black balls have always been a threat.
The blacker your balls
The more blackballed you get
Black males are blackmailed
For just getting upset
Masculinity and jail time
Are sold as a set.
Black fists get blacklisted
Society's Reject
Hope one day my warriors
Get their due respect

The Ugly Duckling

Men will say
"You are so pretty for a dark skin girl."
As if they have shockingly found a beautiful roach
Or an attractive maggot
Or gorgeous pus
Or an exotic curse
As if
that phrase could ever be a compliment
As if "a dark beauty" could be an exception to a rule
The darkness is
the attraction
Not its handicap

Magic Seeds

Her vagina is a tomb covered with dead grass
He plants his seeds in her knowing
Nothing will ever come from their union
She opens her legs
like a pregnant woman preparing for the birth of their miracles
Ignoring the signs
of their barren union.
He gives her flowers
She thinks he is being romantic
He is simply following the rules
of cemeteries
Obligatory petals
For a killing
She might as well be his cum sock and
He might as well be her murderer
He leans over her on their hotel bed as if she's in her casket
He touches her skin softly
Like how mourners stroke a corpse
He tells her "I love you"
She thinks they have a future
But really her vagina is just a tomb
Covered in dead grass
She says "I would leave him if I could" as
She waits for him to visit her again for the next viewing
She has already left herself years ago.
It should be a crime to awaken love in someone you will eat alive
Before they know what bit them
I tell her
Beware of kisses

From men who pledge their devotion without promises of a
tomorrow
He has already killed your future in his mind
He might as well be her murderer.

Romance Story

I did not "call your friend home".
Stop romanticizing murder.
-God.

Once Upon A Time

When someone you love dies
on you
You control your
grief
one day at a time
like an alcoholic controls his addiction.
You feel the
half-filled fuzzy
memories wobbling on the surface of the shelves in your brain
sweet and bitter smelling
but pretty
fermented like cheap 20/20 mad dog liquor.
you walk steady while your head is spinning
like a drunk man walking the line
replaying the moment when the person slipped through the cracks
of your hands
casually
as if he or she were just a replaceable wine glass
Every morning you wake up remembering everything and nothing
Your head throbs while you try to figure out exactly what
happened all the days and nights before.
Grief is an eternal hangover that most do not understand
So many of us try to suppress it and
squash tears like an old beer can and
recycle them
into poems
into smiles

Prince Charming

I used to be the wife of a police man
Sometimes I could taste his last kill on his breath.
One morning, he told me all about this one young man they shot
Casually around our breakfast table over eggs and waffles as he
reached for his orange juice he told me the boy
"reached for his gun or at least that is what it seemed like at the
time."
I didn't have the heart to ask him why he assumed a 13 year old
would have been reaching for a gun.
To be honest, I was scared of him.
He had more guns in the house than shoes
I already know he had no hesitation in using one.
He had a terrible temper.
He busted through our front door each evening as if he were
raiding the place.
Or running a red light during work hours.
He would sniff me and the house like a police dog sniffing a drug
dealer's hideout.
Voice loud like his car's sirens.
He was always so irrationally jealous. I don't know what he
thought he was going to come home and find.
I would never cheat on him
Not because I love him
But because I have seen him get away with murder so I would
never take the risk.
I am so happy that I eventually got away from him two years ago.
Even though it hurt.
I wonder if his second wife can taste my blood on his breath.

I wonder if he will tell her over breakfast that I was "reaching for
another man or a gun or at least that is what it seemed."
All his cop friends came to my funeral
The same cops who never came when my neighbors called 911
after they heard the shots and the screaming.
They all looked somber

My Favorite Superhero

My favorite superhero doesn't have a movie, a comic book, a
merchandising deal or a fancy name.
we simply call him
"Black Man"
he transforms from boy to a savior in our cities faster than a
speeding bullet
supernaturally,
dodging the speeding bullets
all while
carrying his youth on his back
their
tiny arms clasping onto his neck like a soaring brown cape.

The Other Darkness

Margie was tiny, spoiled, and light skin
like the aged powdered parmesan cheese in the back of mama's
cupboard.
She smelled just as bad too but
I was jealous of her.
I was 13.
She was beauty they said and
I was not.
because I was dark.
She lost her virginity when she was eleven.
I remember her telling me how much she felt like a woman when
she had sex.
She was surprised I was untouched.
I wasn't sure if I was chaste or if all the boys in our class thought I
was ugly.
Either way, I didn't want no boys or men on top of me or in me at
the time
though some of her stories were entertaining.
The more I heard the details, the more
I began to love that my skin blended in with the earth and made
me so invisible.
While I was hidden it allowed me to focus only on the inside of me
my other darkness
Years later
I would be curvy
Hot, tasty and
brown-colored like just-cooked
crispy turkey bacon
straight out the cast iron pan

I could feel the men salivating.
everywhere I turned.
I was thankful that I was forced to search for and rely only on
the unseen part of me
Now Margie is pale from stress, cold and looks visibly broken
like frozen Swiss cheese
as she sits in her chair telling me about her latest man.
I am no longer jealous of her.
She tells me she is jealous of me.
and
I feel like both of our skin tones were forcefully held up to a
stainless steel grater
until we were shredded and sore.

Fairy Godfather

"If I don't believe in the daddy who I see everyday, will believing in
a God I never see always be impossible for me? "
-signed a 5 year old incest victim

Black Beauty

Growing up, the only "black beauty" girls were taught about in school was the famous horse in the classic book of the same name. No wonder we all wanted horse hair.

And They All Lived Happily Ever After...

When you commit suicide
You create a six foot wide mural of your dead self on the inside of
your relative's heads.
Our memory of you is never the same.
Every scene we see of you from that point on is you killing yourself
from different angles.
Every memory is framed with the noose we weren't able to loosen
for you.
Your pictures mock us
The smiles now look like crime scenes
Each photo of you looks like a cry for help we couldn't answer.
We notice the sadness in your eyes
too late
so we lay the portraits face down in the den
or under the bed
I know guilt probably doesn't stop someone from killing
themselves
But just in case it does...

Afterword

I always loved fairy tales growing up. Mostly because regardless of unfair, unthinkable, and horrific circumstances, the downtrodden always ended up living "happily ever after" by the end of the story.

Though the tales I read were magical and entertaining, I never saw any of our experiences captured in any of them. I remember cheering when Cinderella and Snow White met their prince and when Rapunzel is able to restore the eyesight of her lover after the spell.

I wondered 'what happens to the stars of black fairy tales when tragedies such as street violence, police brutality, rape, sexual abuse, drug addiction, losing loved ones to murder or suicide replace witches, poisoned apples, and evil step sisters'?

How do we all get to our happily ever after when it hasn't been neatly written for us in our last few lines? Which one of us will take it upon ourselves to be the Fairy Godmothers, fathers, brothers and sisters for all of the youth and community members and for ourselves when we experience the unimaginable? My hope is that each reader asks themselves what their role is in each of these Black Fairy Tales and use their role and their gifts to write all of our happy endings.

-Chin-yer

33975560R00028

Made in the USA
Columbia, SC
14 November 2018